Stikky™ Trees

Stikky™ Trees

LEARN TO RECOGNIZE AT A GLANCE THE 15 MOST COMMON TREES
IN THE UNITED STATES—IN JUST ONE HOUR, GUARANTEED.

LAURENCE HOLT BOOKS
New York

© 2005 Laurence Holt Books, Inc
www.stikky.com

303 Park Avenue South, #1030
New York, NY, 10010

First printing April 2005

Library of Congress Cataloging-in-Publication Data on file.

Cover design and illustrations by Cate Shannon.
Photography by Julian Lawson.

ISBN 1-932974-04-0

10 9 8 7 6 5 4 3 2 1

Printed in Canada

What this book is about

Stikky Trees uses a powerful learning method to teach anyone to identify common trees, step-by-step.

Each step builds on what came before and reinforces it. That way, by the time you reach the end of the book, you will be confident in identifying many of the trees you come across in real life.

Still more exciting, the things you learn will serve as 'hooks' on which you can hang future knowledge.

Along the way, you'll reconnect with our ancestors who would not have gotten far without knowing the trees of the enormous forests around them.

Stikky Trees has four parts:

- **Sequence One** introduces the *top 10 trees* (which, together, account for two-thirds of the trees in the US) and explains the main types of trees—*evergreen* and *deciduous*—and what makes them different. *If possible, you should read this sequence in one sitting.*

- **Sequence Two** builds on what you have learned in Sequence One, tells you how to estimate a tree's age, and how to determine a little of a landscape's history. *Ideally, you should leave a few days, but no more than a week, between completing Sequence One and starting Sequence Two.*

- **The Epilogue**, a special feature of Stikky books, brings together everything you have learned so far and reinforces it in some new and unfamiliar situations. *Again, you should leave a few days between completing Sequence Two and reading the Epilogue.*

- If, by the end of the book, you are eager to find out more, as we hope you will be, you will find dozens of things to explore in the **Next Steps** section.

You can skip to the Next Steps section at any time, of course, but the rest of the book only makes sense if read in order: Sequence One, Sequence Two, Epilogue.

How to read this book

Learning with *Stikky Trees* may be different from how you are used to learning. Please read this page carefully.

First, read Sequence One which runs from the next page to the **Pause point** on page 121. That should take only 30 minutes (but don't worry if it takes longer).

We find people get more out of the book if they stop there and practice what they have learned for real. We'd like you to do the same.

Then, after a few days, read Sequence Two. If you are away from the book for more than a week, you may find it helpful to review some of Sequence One before starting Sequence Two.

To get the most from *Stikky Trees*:

- Relax and take your time
- Don't worry about taking notes
- Don't worry about memorizing anything
- Try to avoid being interrupted.

Most importantly, by turning this page you promise yourself that, when asked a question in the text, you will not flip ahead until you have tried to answer it.

(Flipping backwards to review pages you have already covered is fine.)

Keep this promise and what you learn will stick.

Sequence One

If it weren't for trees,
we would not be able
to breathe.

In fact, we would never have evolved in the first place: trees are the mini oxygen factories that make animal life possible.

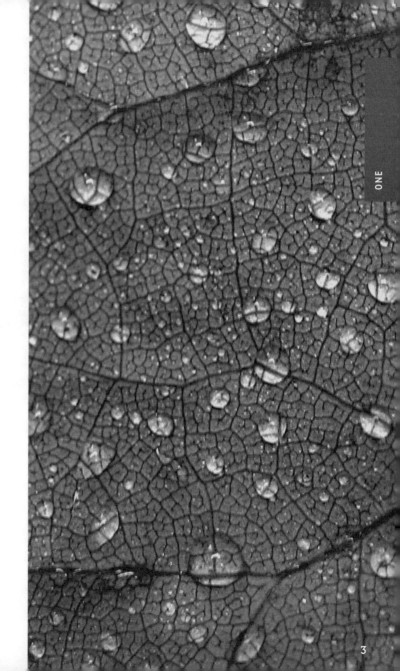

They have been on earth over
300 million years.

(Humans have been on earth
less than 3 million.)

And there are over 300 billion trees in the United States alone.

That's one thousand trees for every person.

From trees we get fruit,
oil, coffee, tea, rubber, and
(of course) the paper you're
holding.

The oldest living thing on
the planet—dated at 5,000
years old—is a tree.

(So is the largest living thing,
but we'll get to that later.)

Our ancestors relied on trees for fuel and to build shelter, so they felled a lot of them.

You would not have gotten far
in the New World (or the Old)
without knowing your trees.

But how many can you identify
today?

About 30 minutes from now
you will recognize plenty.

Ready?

Take a look at these two leaves.

The one at the top is from an oak tree; the one at the bottom is from a maple.

You probably recognize the maple from the Canadian flag, but it's also the most common tree in 16 US states.

The sap of maple trees is used to make maple syrup, a part of the American diet for hundreds of years.

The oak is the most common
tree in 8 states.

Can you tell a maple from
an oak?

Notice that the pattern of veins
in the two leaves is different:
the oak veins are in a fishbone
pattern; maple veins are in a
fan shape.

If you're a <u>fan</u> of <u>maple</u> syrup,
this should be easy to remember.

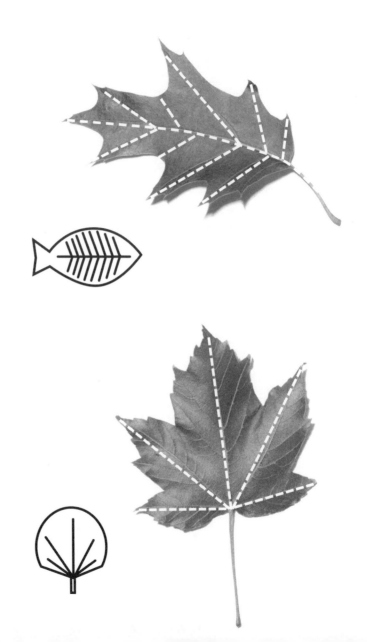

So have you got these two fixed in your mind?

Sure?

Okay, find a maple leaf here.

It's this one.

And find an oak leaf here.

There is either a maple or an oak
leaf here. Your task is to find it
and name it.

Maple.

Too easy? Let's make it more interesting.

This is the leaf from an aspen tree. Aspen leaves are shaped like a spade. (Try remembering it this way: a-spen / a-spade.)

Since aspen leaves dangle from thin stalks, they rustle and shimmer in the slightest breeze. So they're often called "trembling aspens".

This is the leaf of a
sweetgum tree.

You could confuse it with a maple, but the sweetgum is more of a star shape.

Not sweetgum

And this is the leaf from a tupelo tree (like "TOOP-a-low").

Tupelo is the town in Mississippi where Elvis was born.

Its leaf has no teeth, giving it a smooooth edge.

So now we have five leaves.

Tupelo

Oak

Aspen

Maple

Sweetgum

Got them all?

This one—the one with the fan-shaped veins—is a…what?

Maple.

The one shaped like a spade
is a..?

An aspen.

The star-shaped leaf is a..?

Sweetgum.

These leaves with fishbone
veins are..?

Oak leaves.

And the one with the
smooth edge?

Tupelo.

All the leaves we've seen so far are from trees that are called deciduous ("di-SID-you-us"), which means they shed their leaves for the winter.

Got them all?

Sure?

So what tree is this leaf from?

Oak.

And this?

Aspen.

One of these is a tupelo.

Which?

Of course, usually the leaves you are trying to identify will be on a tree, like this.

So what tree do you think this is?

This is an oak tree.

And this?

ONE

Tupelo.

Getting a little harder now.
What tree is this?

An aspen.

Harder. Again, name the tree.

Maple.

One more.

(When you can't tell from a distance, you have to take a closer look.)

Sweetgum.

Great work! If you got all these, you already know five trees.

These two types of tree have needles instead of leaves.

Actually, needles are leaves, just super-thin ones.

These trees are called "evergreen" because they stay green all year round. (Some people think this means they *never* shed their leaves, but if you check beneath a pine tree you'll see that's not true. In fact, they are *always* shedding their leaves.)

Spruce

Pine

Evergreens are tough to tell apart, even close up.

Unless of course you know the trick…

Spruce

Pine

Look very closely at where the
needles are attached to the twig.

If they come in <u>s</u>ingles, it's
a <u>s</u>pruce.

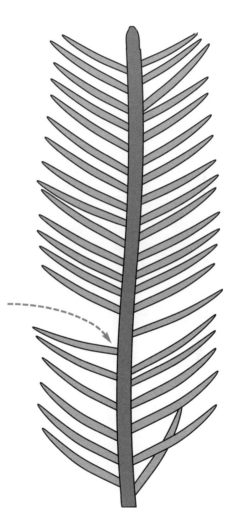

Spruce needles
are attached to
the twig in
singles

If they are plural, like this,
it's a pine.

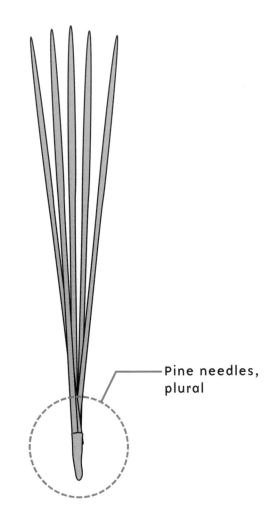

Pine needles,
plural

The bundles of needles on pine trees usually have 2, 3, or 5 needles each.

You have to get pretty close to
tell the difference.

Spruce

Pine

Okay, so what tree does this
twig come from?

Spruce.

And what tree is this?

Pine.

Notice that pine needles are usually a bit longer than those of a spruce.

One odd evergreen doesn't have needles. In fact, it has leaves like no other tree—more like scales than needles.

It's the cedar ("SEE-der").

The cedar tree has a pretty unmistakable shape too.

It's possible to distinguish evergreens from deciduous trees, even from a distance.

For example, there are two groups of trees here, evergreen and deciduous. Which is on the right and which is on the left?

The trees on the right are deciduous (they are aspens).

The trees on the left are evergreen.

Deciduous

Evergreen

Trees like oaks and pines are very common in North America.

In a moment, we'll count down the top 10 most common US trees. But first, a brief recap.

What tree does this leaf come from?

Aspen.

What tree do these needles come from?

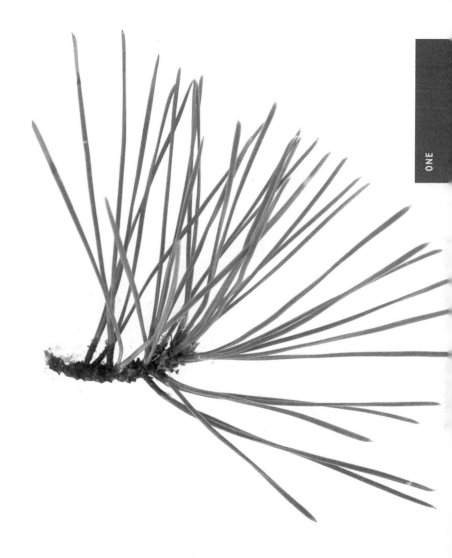

Pine.

What tree is this?

ONE

Tupelo.

ONE

And how about this?

Cedar.

And this tree?

Spruce.

Finally, what tree is this?

Oak.

If you were unsure about any of these, you may want to go back and review.

Okay, now the 10 most common trees in the US.

#10 is a tree you know. Can you name it?

Tupelo.

#9 is the tree on the right in this photo. Can you identify it from it's shape?

Cedar.

#8 is this. What is it?

Spruce.

Remember: single needles, spruce.

And #7 looks like this.

Wait a minute, isn't it a spruce again? It has single needles.

Actually no, it's a Douglas-fir. But it looks so similar that even experts have a tough time telling them apart.

So let's make you into an expert.

Whenever you are confronted by a single-needle tree, there are three possibilities: it's a spruce, it's a Douglas-fir, or it's a fir.

(Yes, firs and Douglas-firs are completely different types of tree. Whoever named them was a little confused, though it's easy to see why.)

To tell the difference between them, here's what you do.

First, find a cone on the tree.

Some trees don't have cones all year round, in which case you are stuck!

But once you have the cone and the needle, it's pretty straightforward.

Douglas-firs are easiest to spot. Their cones have a trident-shaped flag dangling out.

(By the way, Douglas-firs only grow in the western US. But even if you don't live in the west, you may visit, so you need to know how to tell the difference.)

Douglas-fir

Spruce and fir are a bit trickier.

Spruce trees have needles that are <u>s</u>harp and their cones <u>s</u>ag from the branch.

<u>F</u>ir trees have needles that are <u>f</u>lat at the end and their cones <u>f</u>ly up.

(They don't really "fly" up, they point up, but we needed a word beginning with "f".)

Spruce

Fir

So:

- Douglas-firs have dangling trident flags

- Spruces have sharp needles and sagging cones

- Firs have needles that are flat at the end and cones that fly up.

All of them have needles in singles not in plurals.

Okay, let's try some.

What tree is this?

Sagging cone, spruce.

This?

Fir.

And this?

Douglas-fir.

Got it? If you are unsure, feel free to go back over the last few pages. This is about as tough as tree identification gets.

Oh, and do you remember what tree this twig comes from?

It has plural needles, so it's a pine tree.

You don't even need to look at the cone to identify pines.

Okay, so back to the top 10 countdown.

We were at #7. Here it is again. Can you name it now?

Douglas-fir.

#6 you know. What is it?

Sweetgum.

#5 you know too. Go ahead and name it.

Aspen.

America's #4 tree is this. What is it?

Fir.

Now the top three.

They are all trees we already looked at. Here are #3 and #2 together.

Look closely. Can you identify them both?

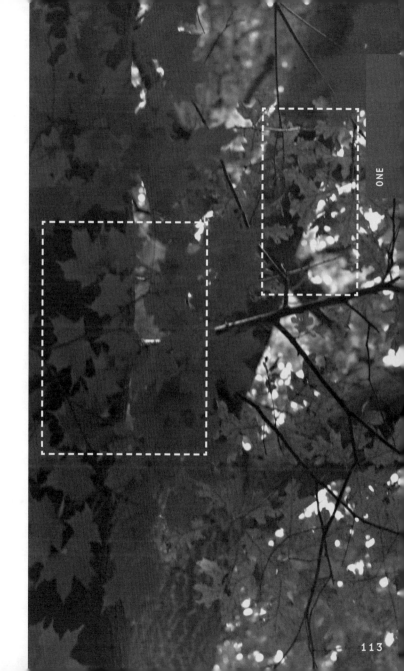

ONE

Maple and oak.

Maple

Oak

So what's left? The #1 most common tree in the US is…

…the pine.

There are over 55 billion of them (55,000,000,000). The pine is the most common tree in 15 states.

Congratulations!

You can now identify the top 10 trees. Together, they account for two-thirds of the trees in the US.

(Incidentally, you can find out what are the top 10 trees in your state by going to the "Insider" section at www.stikky.com/trees.)

ONE

Your new skills will fade unless you try them out on real trees within a week.

If they do fade, just run through this sequence again.

Have fun.

Pause point

To get the most from this book, you should pause after reading this page.

There's much more to come—but be sure to stop here and return to the book a few days later. Here's why.

In the days after you learn something new, your memory fades. You may forget most of what you learned. That might seem annoying, but if you remembered everything you had seen only once, your memory would quickly get overcrowded.

So how do you prevent fading? You need to reinforce what you want to remember. The best way to reinforce knowledge is simple: use it. That's why we recommend going out in the next few days and practicing on real trees.

If you come across trees you don't know, there's a list of places to help you identify them in the Next Steps section on page 229.

Then come back to *Stikky Trees* and start at Sequence Two on the page after this one.

(We have noticed that, when readers continue straight on to Sequence Two, they often get stuck and don't complete it, or find that they forget what they have learned more quickly.)

If you are away from the book for more than a week, or if you don't get a chance to practice in between, you will want to review the end of Sequence One before starting Sequence Two.

When you're ready to continue, read from the next page to the **Pause point** at the end of Sequence Two on page 193.

And remember your promise: when asked a question in the text you will not flip ahead without attempting to answer it.

Sequence Two

Included in this sequence: more of America's top trees, how to tell the age of a tree at a glance, the difference between a leaflet and a leaf, and how to read a landscape's history by its trees.

But first a brief recap.

What tree does this leaf come from?

The aspen.

What about these two?

Tupelo and sweetgum.

(If you're rusty on these, you can always flip back and review Sequence One.)

Tupelo

Sweetgum

What tree is this?

Pine.

Now, how old is this tree?

To figure that out, you need to know that every tree, as long as it's alive, adds a layer to its trunk every year.

Trees never stop getting fatter.

So one way to find a tree's exact age is to cut the tree down and count the rings of growth.

That works, but it's a bit drastic.

Fortunately, there is an alternative. It doesn't give an exact answer, but it's a good estimate...

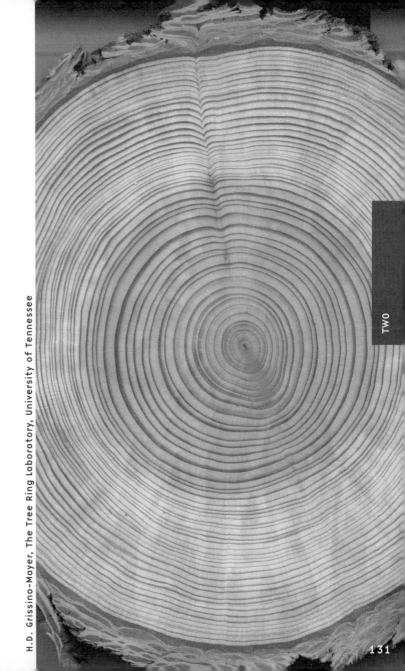

TWO

If you can get your arms around
it, it's about 50 years old.

If it takes two people to get their arms around it, it's about 100 years old.

And, if even two people can't get their arms around it, it's over 100 years old.

This girl is standing about three feet away from the trunk. Do you think she could get her arms all the way around it?

So how old would you say this tree is?

TWO

It's about 100 years old.

And this?

About 50.

And how old do you think this tree is?

100 years? 200? 300?

It's thought to be at least
300 years old.

This tree (which is in New York
City) is known as Hangman's
Elm since traitors were hanged
from it during the Revolution.

So it must have been big then,
230 years ago.

Actually, we haven't looked at elms yet.

Here's an elm leaf.

Elm leaves are easy to spot
because they are uneven at the
base and they have teeth.

(Perhaps they need the teeth to
help fight Dutch Elm Disease.
Sadly, it's a fight they are losing.)

Incidentally, the job of a leaf is simple: to make food for the tree. Each leaf is a small kitchen for photosynthesis (like "photo-SIN-the-sis").

The more sunlight a tree can grab, the more food it can make. Trees are in competition with each other for sunlight.

So trees growing close to each other—in a forest, for instance—race upwards to the light.

Trees growing in the open, though, can afford to spread out to get maximum light.

So when you see an old, spreading tree like this oak, you know it grew up in the open. The forest—if there was one—must already have gone by the time this tree was a sapling.

If leaves make more food the more sunlight they get, why aren't leaves huge?

The problem is, big leaves get torn by the wind.

Some trees get around this by putting lobes on the leaf.

(A "lobe" is a part that sticks out, like the five parts of this maple leaf.)

The gray shading here shows you what the leaf might have looked like before the lobes evolved.

Other trees go further and break one big leaf into several smaller leaflets. The result looks like this. The gray shading shows you what the original leaf might have looked like, before the individual leaflets evolved.

Knowing this can help you identify more trees.

For instance, this is the leaf of an ash tree, made up of seven leaflets.

And this is a leaf from a hickory tree.

Remember, this is one "leaf", several "leaflets".

So how can you tell the difference between ash and hickory?

Well, you might notice that the ash's leaflets are all roughly the same size…

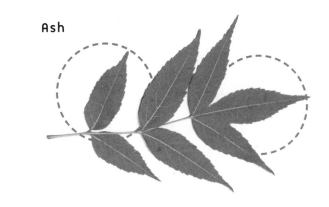

Ash

…while the hickory has some leaflets that are way bigger than the others.

Hickory

Got it?

Then what tree do you think
this is from?

Hickory. The leaflets are way bigger at the tip than at the stem.

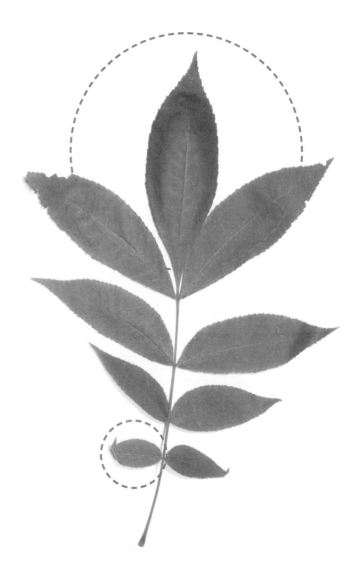

Okay, time for a recap.

What tree do these leaves
come from?

Elm.

What trees are these?

(They're both the same, by
the way.)

Aspens.

(Actually, you could argue that this whole stand of trees is a single organism, since these trees and their neighbors are all clones of a single aspen, joined at the roots.)

What tree is this?

Cedar.

And this?

TWO

Ash.

(If you said "tupelo", remember to
look for leaflets.)

Finally, how old
is this tree?

About 100.

This one person couldn't get their arms around it. But with a friend, they could.

(The dog was a red herring.)

Looking at this tree: do you think it grew in the open or surrounded by other trees?

In the open—its branches are
spread out.

So now we know that this
pasture has been clear of forest
for at least the age of this tree:
100 years.

A single tree can tell you
a lot about the history of
the landscape around you.

Sometimes, the easiest way to identify a tree is by its bark, not by its leaves.

Here is perhaps the most famous bark: the bark of a birch tree which peels off like paper or like a snake shedding its skin (which, in fact, is exactly what the birch is doing).

The bark of most trees is ridged, not wrapped around the trunk like a birch. The ridges result from the bark stretching as the trunk expands, like the Incredible Hulk's ripped clothes.

(This is a maple.)

This tree has pretty distinctive bark too. Can you tell from its leaves what it is?

(Clue: its leaves are made of several leaflets, all the same size.)

Ash.

So now, if you're unsure whether a tree is an ash, you can look for these deep ridges on its bark as confirmation.

You also know the sound this tree's wood makes when a ball hits it. Ash wood has been used to make baseball bats since the Louisville Slugger.

Needle-trees usually have bark in scales like a snake.

Remember this one? What is it?

This is a Douglas-fir tree. (It has trident-shaped flags protruding from its cones.)

What about this?

TWO

Spruce. The cones <u>sag</u>.

And this?

Fir. The cones <u>fl</u>y up.

Here's another single-needle tree (like Douglas-fir, spruce, and fir) that has its signature built in. The hemlock.

Its short needles lie flat on the twig (the other needles we've looked at grow around the twig) and they have two white stripes underneath…

...like the letter "H" for
hemlock.

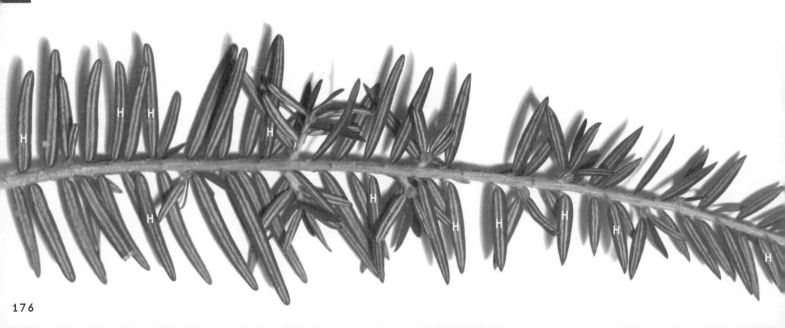

So now, the finale to Sequence
Two. Are you ready? If you're
not sure, feel free to go back
and review.

You know these two evergreens.
What are they?

Pine   Cedar

And these four evergreens, all
with individual needles?

Spruce

Fir

Douglas-fir

Hemlock

What trees do these two leaves come from?

Ash

Hickory

You know this tree from
its bark.

Birch.

Here are two trees that are among the most common in the US. Can you name them?

(This one is tough. Look closely.)

The tree at the top is a maple.
The one at the bottom is an oak.

And here are four different leaves. What trees do they come from?

Elm

Sweetgum

Aspen

Tupelo

Finally, how old is this tree?

About 50.

Six evergreens, nine deciduous trees, plus how to tell their age—you can safely say you know your way around the tall part of the plant kingdom.

With your new skills you should be able to identify many of the trees you come across. Maybe enough to lead your own nature tour.

Remember to practice on real trees within a week, or else your skills will fade.

Pause point

Take a break after reading this page.

As before, you'll get most from this book if you stop here and return a few days later. If you can, get some practice by applying what you've learned on the trees where you live or in a park nearby.

The next section, the Epilogue, recaps everything you have learned so far. It doesn't introduce any new material; instead, it helps you hone your skills.

You know enough by now to find the Next Steps section of interest. It starts on page 229 and has pointers to a variety of resources you can use to build on the hooks you have installed in your head so far.

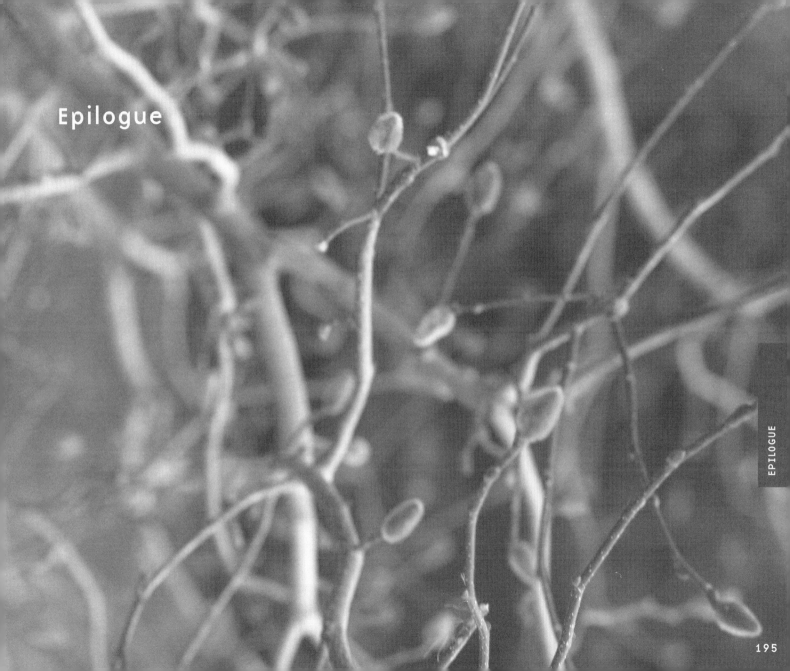

Epilogue

Leaves vary, even on the same tree, to keep you on your toes.

For example, these are from the
same type of tree.

Which tree?

Maple.

(Don't worry about trying to remember the different names, just that they are all maples.)

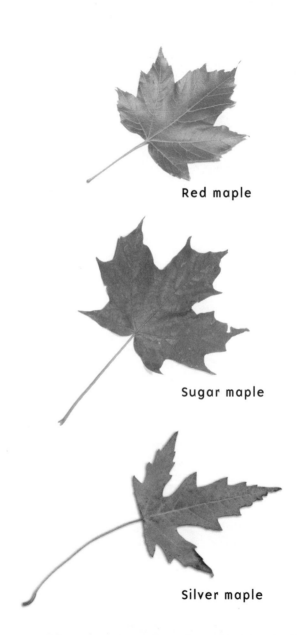

Red maple

Sugar maple

Silver maple

And these are all from one type of tree. Which?

Oak.

Pin oak

Bur oak

White oak

Hybrid oak

Maple, oak…add in the other deciduous trees we've looked at and you have the typical mix found in the northeastern US.

Try naming as many as you can.

In climates—like the northeastern US—that have an inhospitable winter, it doesn't make sense for trees to keep their leaves all year.

That's why deciduous trees drop them.

But in places where the seasons are more constant—such as the western US or way north into Canada, where the climate is always tough—leaves can be kept working all year round. So the most common leaves are evergreen.

How many of these evergreens can you name?

?   ?

?   ?

?   ?

Cedar

Pine

Spruce

Hemlock

Fir

Douglas-fir

In many parts of the US (and also in your local botanical garden, wherever you are), you'll find all of the trees we've looked at.

Of course, trees change depending on when you're looking.

Winter, for instance, can be a tough time for tree identifiers since deciduous trees have no leaves.

(With practice, it's possible to identify them from their shape and their bark.)

But a little detective work sometimes does the trick.

For instance, suppose you found several dead leaves—like the one pictured here—on the ground underneath this tree. What tree would you suspect it to be?

An oak.

The shape helps here too. When oaks have room to grow, they form this distinctive broad, spreading shape.

In spring, some trees produce flowers to attract insects and birds.

(But if they rely on the wind, rather than animals, to spread their pollen, they don't need to waste energy on bright colors.)

In the fall, mature trees produce fruit to scatter their offspring: apples, berries, nuts, and winged samaras. (Officially, all of these are called "fruits".)

Then the tree sucks the precious green chlorophyll ("CLAW-ro-phil") out of its leaves, turning them yellow and red, before they are jettisoned.

Here's a famous tree. How old would you guess it is?

(Notice the size of the man at the center bottom.)

In fact, it is thousands of years old.

This is General Sherman, the world's largest tree, in Sequoia National Park, California.

Not only is it the world's largest tree, it's the world's largest living thing.

Compare it to the largest animal, the blue whale, which typically weighs 100 tons.

General Sherman weighs 2,200 tons!

Okay, now for the grand finale.

Name all eight of the trees these
leaves come from.

Oak

Maple

Sweetgum

Tupelo

Elm

Ash

Hickory

Aspen

And do the same for these six.

217

Spruce

Fir

Douglas-fir

Cedar

Hemlock

Pine

How old
is this tree?

Around 100 years old.

Finally, did this tree originally stand in forest or in the open?

In the open.

If you have read each page up to
this one, you will never look at
a tree the same way again.

World forest coverage 8000 years ago

There is, of course, much more to trees than we had the space to cover. But you have the beginnings of a chart in your head on which to build.

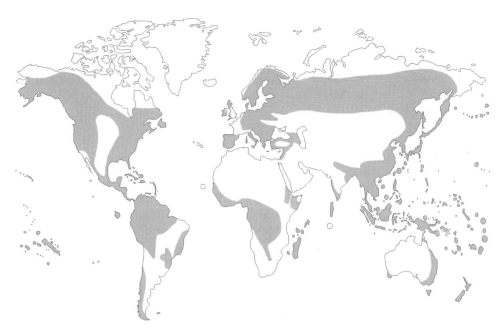

World forest coverage 500 years ago

You have a new connection with
the land we live in.

And that all else lives in.

World forest coverage 100 years ago

Thank you.

World forest coverage today

Next Steps

Now that you know the most common trees, there is much more you can explore. We've included enough here to keep you busy and there is more at www.stikky.com/trees, which is updated frequently.

More trees

Stikky Trees introduced the 15 most common types of tree in the US as a whole (according to the US Forest Service database). But you'll find it helpful to know which of these are common in your area. We've listed the top 10 for each state at www.stikky.com/trees (click on "Insider").

An excellent way to practice identifying trees is to pick an area near where you live—a piece of woodland, a park, or a tree-lined street—and make it a project to name every tree there. It helps to have a pocket guide:

- James Kavanagh's *Pocket Naturalist* is a series of fold-out cards, each featuring over 100 trees local to a single US state. Published by Waterford Press.

- *Northwoods* (www.northwoodsguides.com) publish a set of cards small enough to carry anywhere (one inch by four inches) featuring 36 trees.

- *Fandex: Trees* from Workman Publishing covers 50 trees with several pictures and quite a bit of information for each. The only downside is that you have to have a large pocket.

- Nature Study Guild's *Tree Finder, Winter Tree Finder, Desert Tree Finder*, etc, are mini books that are a little slower to use (you work through a series of questions) but more comprehensive.

You will quickly come across trees we have not covered. Here are some of the easier-to-identify ones that don't make the top 15:

- *Beech*, which has smooth, gray bark that looks a lot like elephant skin. Beech leaves are easily confused with tupelos.

- *Tamarack* (aka Larch) is a less-common needle tree that has lots of needles sprouting from the same point on the twig (rather than just a few, like pines).

- *Flowering Dogwood*, also has smooth-edged leaves but adds white or pink flowers in spring.

- *Willow*, has long, thin leaves (drooping on Weeping Willows).

- *Cherry*, some of whom must have missed the lecture on photosynthesis and so produce deep red leaves instead of green.

- *Sassafras*, wins the prize for the craziest-looking leaf (some look like three-toed feet, others like mittens), used to make tea and root beer.

- *Ginkgo*, runner-up in the crazy leaves contest (its are fan-shaped), used for a herbal remedy supposed to improve memory.

- *Palm* trees are not, according to purists, true trees. Their trunks are not made of real wood, they don't get thicker each year, and they don't branch. They are, perhaps, just large plants.

While we are on the topic of what a tree is: anything shorter than 20 feet is usually considered a shrub though this is a little unfair since they work in the same way as larger trees.

Advanced tree identification

Though we have been talking in terms of 'pines' and 'oaks' there are, of course, several different types of pine and oak: the ponderosa pine, for instance, or the white oak. Technically, 'oak' is the *genus* (pronounced "JEN-us") and 'white oak' is the *species*.

There are over 800 different species of tree in North America and 80,000 worldwide. Again, a good way to learn is to identify every tree in an area you know well. To identify species, you'll need a full field guide (see the next section).

You may be interested to know the top 10 species in the US. Here they are:

1. Red Maple (whose scientific name is *Acer rubrum*, *Acer* is 'maple' and *rubrum* is 'red')

2. Loblolly Pine (*Pinus taeda*)

3. Sweetgum (*Liquidambar styraciflua*)

4. Douglas-fir (*Pseudotsuga menziesii*)

5. Quaking Aspen (*Populus tremuloides*)

6. Sugar Maple (*Acer saccharum*)

7. Balsam Fir (*Abies balsamea*)

8. Flowering Dogwood (*Cornus florida*)

9. Lodgepole Pine (*Pinus contorta*)

10. White Oak (*Quercus alba*)

Field guides

There are several comprehensive field guide **books** on the market, though all seem to be organized for experts, so that it will often take you several minutes to identify a tree:

- Peterson's *Field Guide to Eastern Trees* and *Field Guide to Western Trees* were created before printing color on every page was economically viable, so the color photographs are separated from the descriptions making the guide very difficult to use.

- The *Audubon Society's Field Guides* do the same thing, but make a better fist of the illustrations.

- *Smithsonian Handbooks: Trees* has the distinct advantage of putting color photographs and text descriptions on the same page. But it doesn't tell you much of interest about each tree and it insists on using the Latin names in the key at the front (you have to go to the index for common names).

- *A Natural History of Eastern Trees* and *A Natural History of Western Trees*, both by Donald Culross Peattie, are classics. They aren't really identification guides (they have no color photos, for instance) but connect American history to each species in a unique and fascinating way. Highly recommended.

- The definitive volume in trees is Michael Dirr's 1200-page *Manual of Woody Landscape Plants* which has as much detail as you could want, and then some.

There are also several **online guides** including:

- Eric Haines' identification guide and tree quiz (www.realtimerendering.com/trees/trees.html)

- The National Arbor Day Foundation's *What Tree is That?* (www.arborday.org/trees/treeID.cfm)

- and About.com
  (http://forestry.about.com/cs/treeid/a/tree_id_web.htm).

You may be able to find a tree identification site specific to your local area if you Google your state name and "tree identification". Michigan State University has a thorough example at http://forestry.msu.edu/uptreeid.

How trees work (in a nutshell)

1. Trees make food by the magic of **photosynthesis** in their leaves. Photosynthesis takes carbon dioxide from the air and converts it to carbohydrate (ie, starch). To do this, leaves need sunlight. So the tree, the trunk, the branches, and all are basically a means to get as much sunlight as possible.

2. But there's a problem. Water evaporates through the same holes in the leaves that carbon dioxide comes in through. In fact, a large tree will lose 80 gallons of water a day! Where does all this water come from?

3. The answer is: that's the job of the tree's **roots**. They suck water from the earth. They can usually find enough water near the surface, so roots spread out rather than digging deep into the ground as many people imagine.

4. But the roots have to get the water up to the leaves. So the **trunk** contains a set of very small pipes through which the leaves suck up water. This works well, until air gets in the system which effectively puts a pipe out of action. Since the tree has no way to repair it, it has to make more pipes.

5. So new pipes are made each year and the old pipes are drained and abandoned. This is how the trunk gets fatter: the new pipes are in the new **ring** added to the outside of the trunk (just underneath the **bark**, whose job is to protect the pipes) and the old pipes become the dead wood at the heart of the trunk.

6. All this plumbing takes energy to build and maintain. Where does the energy come from? From the food that the leaves are manufacturing.

There's more to the story (as usual) and an excellent book that tells it is Peter Thomas's *Trees: Their Natural History*.

The five biggest enemies of trees

Trees do not suffer from old age the way animals do. The main living part of a tree—the layer just underneath its bark—is regenerated each year and so is forever young. Instead, trees' main enemies are these five: fire, wind, beavers, disease, and loggers.

With a little ingenuity, you can read the clues in a wooded landscape and figure out which of these five was most recently at work. When you combine this with knowledge about the age of the surviving trees, you can build quite a detailed picture of the history of the area. (This section is based on Tom Wessels superb book *Reading the Forested Landscape*.)

- **Fire**. Though younger trees die, older trees, with larger trunks, often survive fires. They may display large scars at the base where dead leaves burned. (Incidentally, the same scars appear if the tree has been hit by something such as an automobile.) If you can see old trees and young trees but little in between, suspect fire. The young trees may have grown since.

- **Wind**. When trees are blown over their roots pull up a mound of earth. Even years after the trunks have rotted away, the mounds will be visible, with a depression next to them where the tree stood.

- **Beavers**. Stumps left by beavers show evidence of gnawing. There will be a pond and possibly a dam nearby.

- **Disease**. If one species of tree has fallen and others survive, disease is the most likely culprit. Common tree diseases are: beech bark scale disease, Dutch elm disease, white pine blister rust, gypsy moth (attacks *oaks*), and woolly adelgid (*hemlock*).

- **Loggers**. If logging killed the trees, the felled trunks will not be on view. The cut stumps may re-grow, giving rise to multi-trunked trees (though this could also indicate fire or beavers).

Trees are not defenseless to all of these enemies; they have evolved protection such as resin, gum, and latex, to heal over wounds and to keep enemies out. Notice that all of these have sealing properties that humans have found valuable too.

And, occasionally, a tree performs an amazing act of survival. A *ginkgo* tree that grew near the epicenter of the Hiroshima explosion survived and re-grew from its base.

Where new trees come from

If trees want to create offspring, they have to overcome one big problem: they can't move. That means they have to come up with ingenious ways to (a) find a mate and (b) send their progeny off to new ground. Here's how they do it:

1. A tree's equivalent of sperm is pollen. It is usually thrown into the wind in the hope it will land on the female part (the *stigma*) of a nearby tree of the same species. This is rather like trying to send a letter to a friend by making thousands of copies and throwing them from a tall building. Since this is a hit and miss affair, trees produce a lot of pollen. A single birch catkin can contain five million grains. (And so, for some humans, hay fever.)

2. Some trees—the ones that flower in the spring such as *flowering dogwood* and *cherry*—make use of insects to spread their pollen instead of the wind. These trees need to attract the insects, who are suckers for bright petals, scent, and nectar, hence the flowers.

3. In case pollen dispersal—by wind or animal carrier—fails, some trees can fall back on self-pollination as a last resort.

4. Pollen is dispersed in spring and, if successful in arriving at a stigma, the result, sometime later, is a seed. The next problem is to get the seed to fertile new ground.

5. Cone-bearing trees (*pines*, *spruce*, *fir*, etc) simply throw the seed into the wind, the same way they disperse pollen. Other trees wrap the seed up with some food, like a spaceship ready to colonize a new world.

6. There is an enormous variety of these seed spaceships: acorns (from *oak* trees), nuts, fruit (eg, from *apple* trees), winged samaras (little helicopters, from *maples* for example), etc. Technically, all of these are called fruit. They may be scattered by the wind, buried by squirrels, or eaten but not completely digested by birds.

7. The vast majority of seeds perish. One *oak* acorn in a thousand becomes a seedling. And one seedling in a thousand ends the journey as a mature *oak*.

Visiting trees

Botanical gardens and **arboreta** present the ideal opportunity to practice and extend your tree identification skills. They have trees from all around the country (sometime all around the world) and they are, for the most part, labeled. A word of warning, though: if you simply read the labels, you won't learn much. Instead, try to name the tree before looking at its label.

There are over 100 gardens and arboreta in the US. The *American Association of Botanical Gardens and Arboreta* has a searchable database of many—but not all—of them (www.aabga.org). Here are some of the larger ones:

- *Arnold Arboretum of Harvard University*, Jamaica Plain, MA, www.arboretum.harvard.edu
- *Brooklyn Botanic Garden*, www.bbg.org
- *Cornell Plantations*, Ithaca, NY, www.plantations.cornell.edu
- *Dawes Arboretum*, Newark, OH, www.dawesarb.org
- *Denver Botanic Garden*, www.botanicgardens.org
- *Garvan Woodland Gardens*, Hot Springs, AR, www.garvangardens.org
- *Holden Arboretum*, Kirtland, OH www.holdenarb.org
- *Minnesota Landscape Arboretum*, www.arboretum.umn.edu
- *Morris Arboretum*, Philadelphia, PA, www.business-services.upenn.edu/arboretum/
- *Morton Arboretum*, Lisle, IL, www.mortonarb.org
- *Muir Woods National Monument*, Mill Valley, CA, www.visitmuirwoods.com
- *New York Botanical Garden*, Bronx, www.nybg.org
- *North Carolina Arboretum*, Asheville, www.ncarboretum.org
- *Red Butte Garden*, Salt Lake City, UT, www.redbuttegarden.org
- *San Francisco Botanical Garden*, www.strybing.org
- *The Arboretum at Flagstaff*, AZ, www.thearb.org
- *United States Botanical Garden*, Washington, DC, www.usbg.gov
- *United States National Arboretum*, Washington, DC, www.usna.usda.gov
- *University of California Botanical Garden*, Berkeley, http://botanicalgarden.berkeley.edu
- *Washington Park Arboretum*, Seattle, WA, http://depts.washington.edu/wpa

Many university **campuses** have created online maps and walks of their trees and that access to them is free. Google your nearest.

If you'd rather sample a real **forest**, the US Forest Service has detailed information, visitor maps, and links for 150 of them at www.fs.fed.us. Alternatively, try a **national park**: the National Park Service is at www.nps.gov.

If all else fails, you can **grow your own** tree. Several online tree stores will help you figure out which trees are likely to grow well in your climate and soil—and then ship you a sapling (unless your state Department of Agriculture imposes restrictions, as do AK, AZ, CA, HI and others). Try www.arborday.org, www.naturehills.com, or www.historictrees.org (which, somewhat bizarrely, sells descendants of "famous" trees such as a Graceland *sweetgum* and Gettysburg address *honeylocust*).

Stikky recommended websites

There are hundreds of websites related to trees. Here are a few more of our favorites:

- www.americanforests.com, a non-profit, includes the National Register of Big Trees, and *American Forests* magazine

- http://tree.ltrr.arizona.edu, the Laboratory of Tree-Ring Research, will teach you to date

- Both http://plants.usda.gov (the United States Department of Agriculture's Plants Database) and www.hort.uconn.edu/plants (the University of Connecticut Plant Database) include photographs, scientific information, and distribution maps (showing where the tree grows) for just about every US tree

- www.wikipedia, an enormous, free, and surprisingly high quality encyclopedia has dozens of entries on trees.

The 15 Most Common US Trees

Fir

Douglas-fir

Spruce

Pine

Hemlock

Hickory

Ash

Elm

Birch

Sweetgum

Tupelo

Aspen

Cedar

Oak

Maple

The 15 Most Common US Trees

From the book *Stikky Trees*. www.stikky.com
There are two copies of this chart, so you can tear one out and take it with you.

Fir

Douglas-fir

Spruce

Pine

Hemlock

Hickory

Ash

Elm

Birch

Sweetgum

Tupelo

Aspen

Cedar

Oak

Maple

About Stikky books

The Stikky story

We started publishing Stikky books in 2003 after a web-based trial generated far more interest than we expected. Our first book, *Stikky Night Skies*, took a year to create.

The series covers topics we believe will be of value and interest to anyone. We created it because we couldn't find a 'how to' book that took into account recent findings about how people learn. Instead, they often provide too much information and structure it in a way that makes sense to experts but not to beginners. According to our research, most people read less than half of 'how to' books they buy.

The Stikky approach

- Start with small pieces of knowledge and systematically build them into a comprehensive picture
- Make the practice environment as similar as possible to the real world
- Organize the topic around readers' goals such as: How do I read a nutrition label?
- Provide plenty of practice—80% of learning is really re-learning so we stage multiple opportunities to test and reinforce your knowledge
- Make it fun.

How we create a Stikky book

Each book is prepared with the help of subject experts, some of whom are named on the cover. It goes through multiple rounds of review by Test Readers. (If you would like to become a Stikky Test Reader, visit www.stikky.com). We record every time they get stuck, together with hundreds of other suggestions, and make careful changes. Then we go through the whole process again.

Everything about the product in your hands was informed by this research: the format, the binding, even the name. And we only publish a book when we know it works.

Our charity pledge

We promise to spend 10% of profits from the series on knowledge-based charity. We believe that knowledge generates independence and so is a liberating form of aid.

Upcoming Stikky books

Future titles will cover topics such as the secrets of persuasion or playing a musical instrument. If there are topics you would like to see included in the series, suggest them at www.stikky.com, where you will also find news of additions to the series before their publication.

What our readers say

Comments from readers of Stikky books

15 minutes with this book was more valuable than the 3 hours I spent stumbling with another. *BM, USA*

Amazing…so simple and so thorough. *MW, UK*

After running through the sequence, I was able to locate all the points very quickly, can't wait to try it out. *PP, Australia*

Within 30 minutes this book has provided a basis for me to begin a new adventure and hobby. *BR, Indiana*

Yes, my brain is full, and I don't have time to learn anything new. But the folks who created this book are on to something. *A reader from Palo Alto, California*

If you've ever had a teacher who explained things in such a way that they stikk to your mind forever, this book will let you re-live that experience. *SN, New Jersey*

I felt successful from the start. *JC, UK*

This book at first seemed too simple. Then after buying and reading it, I realized it was perfect. The information is presented in such a way that I feel I'll retain the knowledge for life. *A reader from Dallas, Texas*

I have read many, many books on constellations, but this is the most effective one I have ever seen. *WR, Canada*

Now I can observe and understand with confidence. Thank you so much. *LC, Michigan*

Thank you so much for making things so easy. I feel like I've made a start, at long last. *CW, England*

We need more teachers/educators with this approach. *JF, USA*

What a magnificent idea! I will email everybody I know that even MIGHT be interested! Please PLEASE create more of these. *DJ, Ohio*

Beautifully simple, entertaining and delightful. *PL, Ontario*

Thank You

Merry Davis ▪ Robin Everly ▪ Len & Sue Holt ▪ Andrew Lyons ▪ Andrea Magda ▪ Rick Mazzafro
Patrick Miles ▪ Cheryl Oakes ▪ Ryan Sanders ▪ Larry & Kirstin Waddell